She Carries Glory

Embracing Your Calling, Reclaiming Your Power, and Rising in Grace

DEDICATION

To every woman who has ever felt silenced, shattered, or stuck—this is for you.

May these pages remind you that you are not broken beyond repair. You are not too far gone. You are not forgotten. You are a glory carrier. And your light is rising.

To my family—thank you for your patience, love, and unshakable belief in me.

And to my Heavenly Father, whose grace met me in the valley and raised me for the mountaintop—I give You all the glory.

INTRODUCTION

BECOMING A GLORY CARRIER

There's a sacred identity hidden within every woman—the identity of a *glory carrier*. She may not always recognize it, especially if she's been through pain, betrayal, trauma, or loss. But within her lies the power to rise, to rebuild, and to radiate the divine light of purpose.

This book is a journey—an unfolding of chapters that mirror the soul's transformation from wounded to whole, from overlooked to overcomer, from survivor to steward of God's glory. Each chapter is a step forward. A revelation. A healing.

You will find your story in these pages. You'll see your struggles reflected, but more importantly, you'll find strength for your next step. Each section closes with an affirmation, scripture, and reflection prompt—designed to bring your heart closer to truth and your life closer to purpose.

This is more than a book. It is a movement. A declaration. A spiritual invitation to step out of the shadows and into the sacred light of your calling.

You are not just healing. You are becoming. You are not just surviving. You are rising.

Let's begin.

TABLE OF CONTENTS

CHAPTER I

CALLED TO CARRY THE LIGHT

In the quiet moments of the early morning, as the first rays of sunlight gently illuminate the world, I find myself standing at the threshold of a new day. In the stillness of dawn, I am reminded of the power that resides within me the power to shine brightly, to radiate positivity, and to carry the light of glory wherever I go.

I am a glory carrier, a vessel of love and light in a world that sometimes feels dim and uncertain. It is not a title I claim lightly, but one that I have embraced with all my heart and soul. For within me lies a spark, a flame of divine essence that flickers and dances with every beat of my being.

As I take a deep breath and center myself in the present moment, I am reminded of the journey that has led me to this point. The moments of doubt, the challenges faced, and the rejections endured have all shaped me into the person I am today. And through it all, I have learned that true strength lies not in avoiding adversity, but in embracing it with grace and resilience.

I have come to understand that being a glory carrier is not about seeking external validation or approval, but about cultivating a sense of inner peace and self-assurance. It is about recognizing the inherent worth and dignity that resides within me, regardless of the opinions or judgments of others.

In the chapters that follow, I will share the lessons I have learned, the experiences that have shaped me, and the wisdom that has illuminated my path. I will delve into the depths of my soul and explore the essence of what it means to be a glory carrier to embody love, light, and positivity in a world that often seems dark and chaotic.

But for now, as the sun rises higher in the sky and the world awakens to a new day, I stand tall and proud, ready to embrace the challenges and opportunities that lie ahead. For I am a glory carrier, a beacon of hope and inspiration, and I carry the light of glory within me wherever I go.

Affirmation: *I am a beacon of light, radiating love, joy, and positivity to all those around me. I embrace the divine light within me and allow it to shine brightly in every aspect of my life.*

Scripture: "You are the light of the world. A city set on a hill cannot be hidden. Nor do people light a lamp and put it under a basket, but on a stand, and it gives light to all in the house. In the same way, let your light shine before others, so that they may see your good works and give glory to your Father who is in heaven." – *Matthew 5:14-16 (ESV)*

Reflection Prompt: What part of your story are you still hiding in the shadows? Write one way you can let your light shine today right where you are, just as you are.

CHAPTER 2

WRESTLING WITH THE SHADOWS

There are moments in every glory carrier's journey when the shadows of doubt loom large, casting a veil over the light that burns within. It is in these moments of uncertainty and fear that we are tested, where the calling we carry within us is challenged and questioned.

I have walked through valleys of self-doubt and insecurity, where the whispers of inadequacy and fear have threatened to drown out the voice of purpose and passion within me. There have been times when I have faltered, when the weight of expectations and the lure of comfort have led me astray from the path I am meant to walk.

It is a humbling realization to acknowledge that even those who carry the light of glory within them are not immune to moments of darkness and uncertainty. The journey of a glory carrier is not always a straight and steady path; it is filled with twists and turns, highs and lows, moments of clarity and moments of confusion.

In those moments of doubt, I have questioned my worthiness, my abilities, and my purpose. I have wondered if I am truly capable of living up to the calling that has been placed upon my heart. The fear of failure, of falling short of expectations, has gripped me tightly, threatening to extinguish the flame of light that burns within.

But in the midst of the shadows, I have come to realize that doubt is not a sign of weakness, but a testament to the depth of my commitment and the strength of my convictions. It is in the moments of uncertainty that I am called to lean into my faith, to trust in the guidance of a higher power, and to believe in the unique gifts and talents that I possess.

As I navigate the shadows of doubt, I am reminded that walking in my calling is not always easy or straightforward. It requires courage, resilience, and a willingness to confront the fears and insecurities that hold me back. It is a journey of self-discovery and self-acceptance, of learning to embrace both the light and the shadows that reside within me.

And so, as I continue to walk this path of uncertainty and growth, I hold onto the flickering flame of light that burns within me, knowing that even in the darkest of moments, the light of glory will always guide me home.

Affirmation: *I am resilient and strong, capable of overcoming the shadows of doubt that may cloud my mind. I trust in my inner light and wisdom to guide me through moments of uncertainty and fear.*

Scripture: "When I am afraid, I put my trust in you. In God, whose word I praise, in God I trust; I shall not be afraid. What can flesh do to me?" – *Psalm 56:3-4 (ESV)*

Reflection Prompt: Where do shadows of doubt still linger in your life? Write down one area where you will choose to trust God's light over your fear.

CHAPTER 3

AWAKENING THE WARRIOR WITHIN

In reflection and prayer, I feel a stirring deep within my soul, a sense of strength and power that emanates from a source greater than myself. It is in these moments of connection with the Father that I feel the presence of the Lord guiding me, shaping me, and empowering me to step into my true identity.

As I embrace who I am and the calling that has been placed upon my heart, I feel a newfound confidence and assurance growing within me. It is a strength that is not born of my own efforts or abilities, but of the unwavering faith and trust I have in the Lord's plan for my life.

With each step I take on this journey of self-discovery and growth, I feel the power of the Lord infusing me with courage and resilience. The doubts and fears that once held me back begin to fade away, replaced by a deep sense of conviction and purpose.

I no longer question my worthiness or my abilities, for I know that I am a child of God, uniquely created and gifted for a specific purpose. As I surrender to the will of the Lord and align myself with His divine plan, I feel a sense of peace and clarity wash over me, guiding me towards my true calling.

In the moments of uncertainty and challenge, I draw strength from the knowledge that I am not alone on this journey. The Lord walks with me, He talks with me, His mere presence shows up as a source of comfort and strength, empowering me to face whatever obstacles and/or challenges that may come my way.

As I come into my own and embrace the fullness of who I am, I feel the power of the Lord working within me, shaping me into the person He has called me to be. I am filled with a sense of purpose and passion, knowing that as I grow in confidence and faith, the strength of the Lord grows within me.

And so, with each passing day, I continue to walk in the light of His love, feeling the power and strength of the Lord guiding me, empowering me, and leading me towards a future filled with hope, purpose, and divine fulfillment.

Affirmation: *I awaken to my inner strength and courage, embracing the power that lies within me. I am resilient, capable, and ready to face any challenges that come my way with grace and determination.*

Scripture: "I can do all things through him who strengthens me." – *Philippians 4:13 (ESV)*

Reflection Prompt: What divine strength has already been awakened within you? List three ways you've seen yourself grow bolder or stronger in this season.

CHAPTER 4

RISING AS A PRAYER WARRIOR

In the midst of seasons marked by lack and disappointments, I found myself at a crossroads, a moment of reckoning where my faith was tested, and my resolve to praise God through the storms was a strain. It was during these trying times that I embarked on a journey to strengthen my prayer life and embrace the role of a prayer warrior.

As I knelt in prayer, pouring out my heart to the Lord in times of uncertainty and struggle, I felt a sense of peace wash over me. In the stillness of those moments, I discovered the power of prayer—a sacred connection to the divine that transcended earthly challenges and lifted my spirit toward the heavens.

Learning to strengthen my prayer life was not an easy task. It required discipline, commitment, and a willingness to surrender my fears and doubts to the Lord. In the silence of prayer, I found solace and comfort, knowing that God was listening, guiding, and providing me with the strength to endure. Not to be removed because you see I learned that it was the Potters Wheel and I was being molded.

Embracing the role of a prayer warrior was a transformative experience. It meant standing firm in faith, even when faced with adversity, and interceding on behalf of others in times of need. As I lifted my voice in praise and supplication, I felt the presence of the Lord surrounding me, filling me with a sense of purpose and divine empowerment.

During the storms of life, when the winds of doubt and despair threatened to overwhelm me, I learned to praise God through the chaos in spite of what it looked like. I discovered that in the act of worship and thanksgiving, I could find peace and strength to weather the challenges that lay ahead.

As a prayer warrior, I found my voice becoming a beacon of hope and light in the darkness. Through my prayers, I sought to bring comfort to the brokenhearted, healing to the wounded, and restoration to the weary souls who crossed my path.

And so, as I continued on this journey of faith and prayer, I embraced the role of a prayer warrior with humility and reverence. I learned to trust in the Lord's plan, to praise Him through the storms, and to stand firm in the knowledge that His grace and mercy would carry me through every trial and tribulation because they were sufficient.

In those times of prayer and reflection, I found strength, courage, and a deep sense of peace, knowing that as a prayer warrior, I was called to be a vessel of God's love and light in a world that often feels lost and broken.

Affirmation: *I am a prayer warrior, standing in faith and interceding with power and purpose. My prayers are a source of light, love, and healing for myself and others, making a meaningful impact in the spiritual realm.*

Scripture: "Therefore confess your sins to each other and pray for each other so that you may be healed. The prayer of a righteous person is powerful and effective." – *James 5:16 (NIV)*

Reflection Prompt: What areas of your life, or the lives of others are you being called to pray over with boldness and faith today?

CHAPTER 5

THE SACRED ART OF HEARING GOD

In the pit of my sanctified soul, I began to cultivate a deep sense of confidence in hearing God's voice and the ability to pivot timely as He gave direction. It was a journey marked by moments of clarity, whispers of wisdom, and the gentle nudges of divine guidance that shaped my path in profound ways.

As I sought to tune my ears to the voice of God, I discovered that His guidance often came in subtle ways, through a quiet intuition, a sudden inspiration, or a profound sense of knowing that transcended logic and reason. Learning to discern His voice amidst the noise of the world required patience, practice, and a deepening of my faith.

With each step I took in faith and obedience, I found that God's direction was always timely and precise. His guidance was like a compass, pointing me towards the paths of righteousness, wisdom, and purpose. In those moments of decision and uncertainty, I learned to trust in His voice and pivot swiftly as He directed my steps.

The ability to pivot timely as God gave direction was a skill that required surrender and humility. It meant setting aside my own plans and desires, and aligning my will with His divine purpose. As I embraced this posture of openness and receptivity, I found that God's guidance flowed freely and effortlessly, leading me towards greater clarity and alignment with His will.

Through the art of divine guidance, I discovered that God's voice was not limited to grand proclamations or dramatic revelations. It was often found in the quiet whispers of the heart, the gentle tugs of intuition, and the subtle signs that pointed me towards His perfect will.

As I honed my ability to hear God's voice and pivot timely as He gave direction, I found a deep sense of peace and confidence in the knowledge that I was never alone on this journey. His presence was a constant source of comfort and assurance, guiding me through the twists and turns of life with grace and wisdom.

And so, with each passing day, I continued to walk in faith and obedience, knowing that as I listened to God's voice and pivoted timely as He gave direction, I was following the path He had laid out for me, a path filled with purpose, meaning, and divine fulfillment.

Affirmation: *I trust in the divine guidance that leads me on my path. I am open to receiving wisdom, clarity, and direction from the higher power that guides my steps with grace and purpose.*

Scripture: "Trust in the Lord with all your heart and lean not on your own understanding; in all your ways submit to him, and he will make your paths straight." – *Proverbs 3:5–6 (NIV)*

Reflection Prompt: When was the last time you sensed God nudging you in a direction you didn't expect? What would it look like to respond with immediate obedience the next time?

CHAPTER 6

SHATTERING THE LIE OF NOT ENOUGH

As I embarked on the journey of opening myself up and tearing down the walls I had built from the physical abuse I endured, I found myself confronted with a deep sense of unworthiness and self-doubt. The scars of the past had left me feeling broken and undeserving of the love and power that the Lord was bestowing upon me.

The wounds of physical abuse had seeped deep into my soul, leaving behind a residue of shame and guilt that clouded my perception of self-worth. I struggled to reconcile the gifts and blessings that the Lord was pouring into my life with the belief that I was unworthy of such grace.

In my darkest moments, I pushed everything deep down inside, burying the pain and trauma beneath layers of self-denial and self-criticism. I convinced myself that I didn't deserve the path of peace and healing that the Lord had laid before me, that I was unworthy of the light that shone upon me.

As I walked the path of faith and healing, I felt like a fraud, living a life and walking a path that I believed I did not deserve. The weight of self-doubt and inadequacy pressed down upon me, threatening to extinguish the flickering flame of hope and redemption within me.

But as I journeyed deeper into the recesses of my soul, I began to confront the lies and distortions that had taken root in my heart. I realized that the wounds of the past did not define me, that the scars I carried were not a reflection of my worth or value in the eyes of the Lord.

Slowly, with each step towards self-acceptance and forgiveness, I began to peel back the layers of self-doubt and shame, allowing the light of truth and grace to penetrate the darkness within me. I embraced the reality that I was a child of God, loved and cherished beyond measure, deserving of His mercy and compassion.

In the darkness of my brokenness, I found solace in the arms of the Lord, who whispered words of love and acceptance, who cradled me in His embrace and lifted me up from the depths of despair. I learned that true worthiness is not earned through perfection or achievement, but through the unconditional love and grace of the Lord.

And so, as I embraced my true identity as a beloved child of God, I let go of the self-imposed limitations and embraced the path of peace and healing that had been bestowed upon me. I walked forward with courage and faith, knowing that I was worthy of the love and power that the Lord had given me, and that I was deserving of the blessings that awaited me on this journey of redemption and grace.

Affirmation: *I release self-doubt and embrace self-confidence. I am worthy, capable, and deserving of all the good that comes my way. I trust in my abilities and believe in my inner strength.*

Scripture: "For God gave us a spirit not of fear but of power and love and self-control." – *2 Timothy 1:7 (ESV)*

Reflection Prompt: What false belief about yourself have you been carrying? Write a truth from God's Word to replace it, and speak it aloud daily this week.

CHAPTER 7

FROM HIDING TO RADIATING

As I emerged from the shadows of self-doubt and fear, I made a conscious decision to come out of hiding and move forward, stepping into the forefront of my life with a renewed sense of purpose and faith. Despite my lingering self-doubt and uncertainty, I chose to give God my all, trusting in His kindness and grace to guide me on this journey of self-discovery and redemption.

The path of stepping into the light was not easy, filled with moments of hesitation and trepidation. I grappled with my own insecurities and fears, questioning whether I was truly worthy of the blessings and opportunities that lay before me. But in the midst of my doubts, I felt a gentle nudge from the Lord, urging me to trust in His plan and to surrender to His will

With a heart full of gratitude and humility, I took a bold step forward, stepping into the forefront of my life with a newfound sense of courage and determination. I embraced the challenges and uncertainties that lay ahead, knowing that God's kindness and love would sustain me through every trial and triumph.

As I gave God my all, even in the midst of my self-doubt, I experienced a profound sense of peace and reassurance. His presence enveloped me like a warm embrace, dispelling the shadows of doubt and filling me with a deep sense of purpose and belonging.

I discovered that God's kindness knows no bounds, that His love is unconditional and unwavering. In moments of weakness and vulnerability, He was my rock and my refuge, guiding me with gentle hands and leading me towards a future filled with hope and promise.

With each passing day, I learned to lean into God's kindness, allowing His grace to permeate every aspect of my life. I found the strength to overcome self-doubt and insecurities, stepping boldly into the light of His love and mercy.

And so, as I continued on this journey of faith and self-discovery, I embraced the truth that God had been kind to me, showering me with His blessings and guiding me with His wisdom. I walked forward with confidence and trust, knowing that His kindness would lead me towards a future filled with purpose, joy, and divine fulfillment.

Affirmation: *I step into the light with courage, grace, and confidence. I embrace the truth within me and let my light shine brightly for all to see.*

Scripture: "The Lord is my light and my salvation; whom shall I fear? The Lord is the stronghold of my life; of whom shall I be afraid?" – *Psalm 27:1 (ESV)*

Reflection Prompt: What part of your purpose have you been hiding from? How would your life change if you boldly stepped into the light today?

CHAPTER 8

RESTORING CONFIDENCE AFTER THE STORM

The effects of abuse can be deeply damaging, tearing down one's confidence and casting a shadow of doubt over every step and decision. The scars left behind by abuse can permeate every aspect of a person's life, creating a pervasive sense of fear, insecurity, and self-doubt.

Abuse shatters not only the physical body but also the spirit and sense of self-worth. It instills a profound sense of powerlessness and erodes the belief in one's own abilities and judgment. Survivors of abuse often find themselves second-guessing every decision, questioning their worth, and struggling to trust themselves and others.

The trauma of abuse lingers long after the physical wounds have healed, manifesting in emotional scars that impact every aspect of life. The constant fear of making a wrong move or trusting the wrong person can paralyze survivors, making it difficult to move forward with confidence and clarity.

The insidious nature of abuse can plant seeds of self-doubt that take root deep within the psyche, causing survivors to question their own perceptions and instincts. The manipulation and gaslighting that often accompany abuse can distort reality and create a distorted sense of self, leading to a cycle of self-blame and doubt.

Rebuilding confidence after abuse is a challenging and often painful process. It requires survivors to confront their past traumas, process their emotions, and challenge the negative beliefs that have been internalized. It involves seeking support from trusted individuals, therapy, and self-care practices to heal from the wounds of the past and reclaim a sense of agency and self-worth.

Through therapy, self-reflection, and support from others, survivors can begin to rebuild their confidence and trust in themselves. They can learn to set boundaries, listen to their intuition, and make decisions that align with their values and goals. It is a journey of self-discovery and empowerment, reclaiming one's voice and agency in the face of past trauma.

As survivors of abuse begin to heal and rebuild their confidence, they can gradually regain a sense of control over their lives and move forward with a renewed sense of purpose and self-assurance. It is a journey of resilience, strength, and courage, as survivors reclaim their power and rewrite their own narrative beyond the shadows of abuse.

Affirmation: *I am worthy of love, respect, and healing. I release the pain of the past and rebuild my confidence with strength and resilience. I am a survivor, not a victim, and I deserve to thrive.*

Scripture: "The Lord is close to the brokenhearted and saves those who are crushed in spirit." – *Psalm 34:18 (NIV)*

Reflection Prompt: In what ways has your confidence been shaken by past pain? Write one truth about yourself that you will hold onto as you rebuild your confidence.

CHAPTER 9

PURPOSE IN THE MIDST OF PAIN

Walking in a God-given assignment can be a daunting task, especially when one is grappling with brokenness and wounds from the past. The journey of fulfilling a divine purpose becomes even more challenging when the weight of past traumas and struggles weighs heavily on the soul.

The difficulty lies in finding the strength and courage to step into the calling that God has placed upon one's life, despite feeling shattered and fragile. The brokenness within can create barriers to embracing the assignment, leading to self-doubt, fear, and a sense of unworthiness.

Navigating the path of a God-given assignment requires vulnerability and a willingness to confront the wounds that have shaped one's identity. It means facing the pain, acknowledging the broken pieces, and allowing God's healing touch to mend the shattered parts of the soul.

The struggle of walking in God's assignment when broken is multifaceted. It involves battling the inner voices of self-criticism and inadequacy, overcoming the fear of failure and rejection, and finding the faith to trust in God's plan despite the uncertainties that lie ahead.

The brokenness can cloud one's vision, making it challenging to see the path that God has laid out. It can create barriers to hearing His voice clearly, leading to confusion and hesitation in moving forward with conviction and purpose.

However, amidst the brokenness and struggles, there is hope. God's grace is sufficient to meet us in our weakness and His strength is made perfect in our brokenness. He can use our scars and vulnerabilities to bring forth beauty and purpose in ways we may never have imagined.

Walking in a God-given assignment when broken requires a deep reliance on God's power and grace. It involves surrendering our brokenness to Him, allowing Him to work through our weaknesses and transform them into sources of strength and resilience.

As we lean on God's promises and trust in His unfailing love, we can find the courage to step into the assignment He has prepared for us, even in the midst of brokenness. It is a journey of faith, perseverance, and surrender, as we allow God to heal our brokenness and lead us towards a future filled with hope and divine fulfillment.

Affirmation: *Even in my brokenness, I trust in God's plan for me. I walk in His assignment with faith and perseverance, knowing that He will heal my wounds and strengthen me for the journey ahead.*

Scripture: "But he said to me, 'My grace is sufficient for you, for my power is made perfect in weakness.' Therefore I will boast all the more gladly about my weaknesses, so that Christ's power may rest on me." – *2 Corinthians 12:9 (NIV)*

Reflection Prompt: What pain from your past has kept you from fully stepping into your assignment? Invite God into that place today and write a prayer of surrender and trust.

CHAPTER 10

HEALING THROUGH HEAVEN'S EYES

As the journey of healing unfolds, a profound shift in perspective begins to take shape. Gaining perspective while healing is a transformative process that allows for a deeper understanding of the past, a renewed appreciation for the present, and a hopeful outlook toward the future.

Healing is not simply about physical recovery; it is a holistic journey that encompasses emotional, mental, and spiritual well-being. As wounds are tended to and scars begin to fade, a new clarity emerges, offering a fresh lens and mindset shift on the view of the land.

Through the process of healing, old wounds are revisited and reexamined with a compassionate eye. Instead of being sources of pain and anguish, they become opportunities for growth and resilience. Each step toward healing brings a new layer of understanding and acceptance, allowing for a shift in perspective that is both liberating and empowering.

Perspective is gained through the introspection and self-discovery that accompany healing. As the layers of hurt and trauma are peeled back, a deeper awareness of one's own strengths, vulnerabilities, and resilience emerges. This newfound perspective offers insight into the ways in which past experiences have shaped and molded the individual, leading to a greater sense of self-awareness and compassion.

Healing also brings a heightened appreciation for the present moment. As the weight of the past begins to lift, the beauty and wonder of the present become more vivid and vibrant. Each moment is savored, each experience is cherished, and each interaction is infused with gratitude and mindfulness.

Looking toward the future, gaining perspective through healing opens up a world of possibilities and potential. The scars of the past no longer define or limit, but instead serve as reminders of strength, courage, and resilience. The future is seen through a lens of hope and possibility, with the knowledge that healing is an ongoing journey that paves the way for growth and transformation.

Ultimately, gaining perspective while healing is a journey of self-discovery, empowerment, and renewal. It is a process of embracing the past with compassion, living in the present with gratitude, and looking toward the future with hope and optimism. Through healing, perspective is gained, wisdom is cultivated, and the journey toward wholeness and well-being continues to unfold with grace and resilience.

Affirmation: *Through healing, I embrace a new perspective filled with compassion, understanding, and gratitude. I release the past and open my heart to the beauty of growth and transformation.*

Scripture: "He heals the brokenhearted and binds up their wounds." – *Psalm 147:3 (ESV)*

Reflection Prompt: Think back to a painful experience that once defined you. How has your perspective on that moment changed since beginning your healing journey?

CHAPTER 11

THE FREEDOM OF FORGIVENESS

A s the path to healing and gaining perspective continues to unfold, one of the most powerful and transformative aspects that often emerges is the practice of forgiveness and release. Forgiveness is a profound act of grace and compassion that can bring deep healing and liberation, both to oneself and to others.

Self-Forgiveness: One of the most important steps in the healing process is learning to forgive oneself. Often, we carry guilt, shame, and self-blame for past mistakes or perceived shortcomings. Through self-forgiveness, we can release ourselves from the burden of the past and embrace a sense of self-compassion and acceptance.

Forgiveness of Others: Forgiving those who have caused us pain or harm is a challenging but essential part of the healing journey. It involves letting go of resentment, anger, and bitterness towards others, and choosing to extend grace and understanding instead. Forgiveness is not about excusing the actions of others but about releasing the hold that those actions have on our hearts and minds.

Healing Relationships: Through the practice of forgiveness, relationships can be healed and restored. When we release grudges and resentments towards others, we create space for reconciliation, understanding, and compassion. Forgiveness can pave the way for deeper connections and healthier dynamics in our relationships.

Release of Emotional Baggage: Holding onto past hurts and grievances can weigh us down emotionally and spiritually. By practicing forgiveness and release, we unburden ourselves from the emotional baggage that hinders our growth and well-being. Letting go allows us to move forward with greater lightness and freedom.

Cultivating Compassion: Forgiveness is an expression of compassion towards oneself and others. It involves seeing beyond the actions and behaviors that have caused pain and recognizing the humanity and inherent worth of all individuals. Through forgiveness, we cultivate empathy, kindness, and understanding towards ourselves and those around us.

Embracing Peace: Forgiveness is a pathway to inner peace and serenity. When we release the grip of past grievances and choose forgiveness, we create space for peace to enter our hearts and minds. Letting go of resentment and anger allows us to experience a sense of calm and tranquility that transcends the challenges of the past.

Spiritual Growth: Forgiveness is also a spiritual practice that deepens our connection with the divine. It aligns us with the principles of grace, mercy, and love that are central to many spiritual traditions. Through forgiveness, we open ourselves to the transformative power of divine love and healing.

In embracing forgiveness and release, we not only heal ourselves but also create a ripple effect of healing and transformation in our lives and the lives of those around us. It is a courageous and transformative act that leads us towards greater wholeness, peace, and spiritual growth.

Affirmation: *I choose to embrace forgiveness and release the weight of resentment and bitterness. Through forgiveness, I set myself free and open my heart to peace, love, and joy.*

Scripture: "Bear with each other and forgive one another if any of you has a grievance against someone. Forgive as the Lord forgave you." – *Colossians 3:13 (NIV)*

Reflection Prompt: Who do you need to forgive, including yourself? Write a release statement as a symbolic act of letting go and opening your heart to peace.

CHAPTER 12

ANCHORED IN GRACE

As we go deeper into the depths of healing, forgiveness, and self-discovery, we arrive at a place of profound significance, standing in grace, fully embracing our calling as a glory carrier. It is a moment of divine alignment, where the threads of our past struggles and triumphs weave together to form a tapestry of purpose and meaning.

By grace, we stand tall, rooted in the knowledge that we are chosen vessels of light and love, called to shine brightly in a world that often feels dim and uncertain. The grace that surrounds us is not earned through our efforts or achievements but bestowed upon us as a gift from the divine, a reflection of His boundless mercy and compassion.

In this sacred space of grace, we find the strength to fully embody our calling as glory carriers. We stand firm in our truth, embracing our authenticity and inner light with unwavering faith and courage. It is a moment of empowerment, where we realize that our past wounds and struggles have prepared us to radiate grace and compassion to those in need.

Standing in grace, we are reminded of the transformative power of forgiveness and release. The burdens of the past have been lifted, replaced by a sense of liberation and freedom that allows us to move forward with clarity and purpose. We no longer carry the weight of shame or guilt but walk in the light of divine love and acceptance.

As glory carriers, we are called to be beacons of hope and inspiration, spreading joy, positivity, and love wherever we go. Our presence is a testament to the grace and mercy that have guided us on this journey of healing and self-discovery. We stand as living testimonies to the transformative power of faith, resilience, and unwavering belief in the goodness of the divine.

In the stillness of grace, we find the courage to step boldly into our calling, knowing that we are supported by a higher power that guides our every move. We stand as vessels of light, illuminating the path for others and leading by example through our actions, words, and deeds.

Standing in grace, we embody the essence of a glory carrier, a beacon of hope, a source of inspiration, and a reflection of divine love. As we continue on this journey of faith and purpose, we stand united in our mission to spread light and positivity, knowing that we are upheld by the grace of the divine and empowered to make a difference in the world.

Affirmation: *I stand in grace, knowing that I am loved, accepted, and forgiven. I walk in faith and humility, trusting in God's unending grace to guide me through every challenge and triumph.*

Scripture: "But he gives us more grace. That is why Scripture says: 'God opposes the proud but shows favor to the humble.'" – *James 4:6 (NIV)*

Reflection Prompt: What does standing in grace mean to you right now? Reflect on how grace has sustained you, and write down a declaration of the truth you now stand in.

CHAPTER 13

WHEN PROPHECY BECOMES REALITY

Now, as we stand in grace, fully embracing our calling as glory carriers, we find ourselves at a pivotal moment of profound significance, the fulfillment of prophecy. The seeds of destiny that were planted within us are now blossoming into reality, and we are witnessing the divine plan unfold before our eyes.

The trek toward the fulfillment of prophecy is a testament to faith, perseverance, and an unwavering belief in the promises of the divine. It is a path marked by moments of challenge, growth, and transformation as we navigate the twists and turns of life guided by the hand of destiny.

With each step we take, we move closer to the realization of the prophecies that have been spoken over our lives. The words of hope, purpose, and blessing that were whispered in the depths of our souls are now manifesting in tangible ways, shaping the course of our journey and illuminating the path ahead.

The fulfillment of prophecy is a sacred and awe-inspiring moment, where we witness the alignment of our lives with the divine plan. It is a reminder that we are co-creators of our destiny, working in harmony with God to bring about the fulfillment of our highest potential and purpose. Don't confuse doing the work with helping God, as He needs no help. As we work with God our only expectation is to follow the steps He has ordered for us to follow.

As the prophecy comes to fruition, we are filled with a sense of awe and gratitude for the grace and mercy that have guided us on this journey. We reflect on the challenges we have overcome, the lessons we have learned, and the growth we have experienced along the way, knowing that each step has been a necessary part of the divine plan.

The fulfillment of prophecy is a testament to the power of faith and belief in the unseen. It is a reminder that even in the face of doubt and uncertainty, we can trust in the promises of the divine and hold fast to the vision of a future filled with abundance, joy, and divine favor.

As we stand on the threshold of the fulfillment of prophecy, we embrace the journey with open hearts and minds, ready to receive the blessings and miracles that await us. We walk forward with confidence, knowing that we are guided by a higher power and supported by heaven in bringing to fruition the prophecies that have been spoken over our lives.

In the fulfillment of prophecy, we find validation, purpose, and a deep sense of alignment with the divine will. It is a moment of celebration, gratitude, and awe as we witness the unfolding of destiny and the realization of our highest calling as glory carriers.

Affirmation: *I embrace the fulfillment of prophecy in my life with faith and gratitude. I trust in God's divine plan and purpose for me, knowing that every promise will come to pass in His perfect timing.*

Scripture: "For no matter how many promises God has made, they are 'Yes' in Christ. And so through him the 'Amen' is spoken by us to the glory of God." – *2 Corinthians 1:20 (NIV)*

Reflection Prompt: What promise from God are you now beginning to see take root or blossom in your life? Journal about how you'll continue walking in alignment as that prophecy unfolds.

CHAPTER 14

PURPOSE IN EVERY PLACE

"When Calling Meets Career"

There is a sacred harmony that emerges when every part of your life begins to reflect the purpose God placed within you. No longer divided between who you are in the sanctuary and who you are in the boardroom, you begin to walk in a seamless alignment where your faith informs your function, and your calling enhances your career.

I stand today in a divine intersection, a meeting place of destiny where my corporate life and spiritual walk no longer compete but *collaborate.*

In the professional world, I show up with excellence, strategy, and vision. I lead teams, manage responsibilities, and chase after measurable goals. Yet every skill I employ and every decision I make is now infused with something greater: a divine directive. The wisdom I once sought only in data and deadlines is now drawn from the well of prayer, discernment, and kingdom values.

I used to compartmentalize these parts of my life. I was one person in the boardroom and another in my prayer closet. But grace has taught me that I don't have to choose one or the other. *I am both.*

This is alignment.

When your calling walks into your 9-to-5. When your values echo through your business meetings. When your leadership becomes a ministry in motion. When the work of your hands becomes an extension of the worship in your heart.

I no longer see my corporate role as separate from my faith, it's a platform for it.

Spiritual Reflection

God is a God of order and alignment. He doesn't just call you to a place, He aligns your gifts, your passions, and your past experiences to prepare you for it. The world may chase balance, but the kingdom calls us to *alignment*, a life where our spiritual identity and professional influence merge to fulfill divine purpose.

Proverbs 16:9 says, *"The heart of man plans his way, but the Lord establishes his steps."* This verse isn't a limitation, it's a liberation. It means that while we strategize, God orchestrates. While we dream, He designs. And when we submit our vision to His will, He aligns us with opportunities we could never have imagined.

Alignment is not ease, it is *elevation.* It's God saying, *"You're not just placed here. You're positioned."*

Affirmation

I align my heart, mind, and actions with God's purpose for my life. I walk in divine alignment, trusting that He orders my steps and uses every part of my life, both spiritual and professional, for His glory.

Scripture Reflection

"The heart of man plans his way, but the Lord establishes his steps."
– *Proverbs 16:9 (ESV)*

Reflection Prompt

Where in your life have you felt a disconnect between your faith and your function? Journal about how God may be inviting you to align these areas. What does it look like for your career to serve your calling, and for your calling to elevate your career?

CHAPTER 15

THE GIFT OF A NEW DAY

"A Fresh Start with Every Sunrise"

There is something sacred about the sunrise, a declaration that no matter what yesterday held, today begins again. Each dawn brings with it the tender assurance of heaven: *You are not forgotten, you are not finished, and My mercies are new.*

This is the grace we wake up to. Not because we earned it. Not because we have it all together. But because God, in His unchanging faithfulness, chooses to extend it again and again.

Every day is a canvas of possibility.

Every breath is an invitation into presence.

Every sunrise is an echo of redemption.

As I look back on this entire journey, the healing, the struggle, the standing, the rising, I realize that it is the daily mercies of God that have carried me. Not just through the big moments of breakthrough, but through the ordinary, quiet days when I wasn't sure I had the strength to keep going. His mercies met me there.

And they still do.

Spiritual Reflection

Lamentations 3:22–23 reminds us, *"The steadfast love of the Lord never ceases; his mercies never come to an end; they are new every morning; great is your faithfulness."* These words are not poetic wishful thinking, they are a divine promise. A reassurance that even when we fall short, even when the path feels unclear, God is still faithful.

To embrace new mercies every day is to walk in a rhythm of release and renewal. It means choosing to let go of yesterday's regrets and walk boldly into today's possibilities. It is trusting that grace not only covers your past, but *fuels* your future.

This evolution of becoming a glory carrier, of reclaiming your light, of rising in purpose and standing in grace, it's not a one-time transformation. It's a *daily invitation.* To show up. To grow deeper. To choose joy. To forgive again. To believe again.

Each new mercy reminds us:
You are still becoming.
You are still called.
You are still covered.

Affirmation

I embrace new mercies every day with gratitude and hope. I let go of yesterday's mistakes and shortcomings, knowing that each day is a fresh start filled with God's compassion and grace. I walk in the promise of new beginnings.

Scripture Reflection

"The steadfast love of the Lord never ceases; his mercies never come to an end; they are new every morning; great is your faithfulness."
– *Lamentations 3:22–23 (ESV)*

Reflection Prompt

As you reflect on your own journey, what new mercy do you need to receive today? Write a letter to yourself from the voice of grace, a letter that releases yesterday and welcomes today. Speak to your heart with compassion, reminding yourself of what God sees in you right now.

A FINAL WORD

THE JOURNEY CONTINUES

Dear reader, this book may be closing, but your story is just beginning.

You have walked through healing. You have faced the shadows. You have stood in grace and purpose. And now, you rise daily, with fresh mercies, renewed vision, and divine fire in your soul.

You are a *glory carrier.*

You are a light in dark places. A vessel of love. A reflection of heaven's resilience.

Let this be your daily prayer:

"Lord, help me rise with new mercies. Help me walk with open hands, open heart, and open eyes, ready to see You in every moment, ready to love without limit, ready to live boldly in the purpose You designed for me."

The journey is not over.

It's unfolding with every sunrise.

CLOSING PRAYER

A BENEDICTION FOR THE GLORY CARRIER

Father God,

Thank You for every heart that has turned these pages and dared to believe again. For every woman who has faced darkness and still chose the light, for her, Lord, I ask for divine strength, peace, and unshakable purpose.

Let Your glory rest upon her. Let Your voice rise within her. Let Your Spirit guide her steps.

May she walk boldly in her calling, trusting not in her perfection, but in Your presence. May every scar become a story of Your faithfulness. May every day be filled with new mercies and divine appointments.

Make her a glory carrier, radiant, redeemed, and released.

In Jesus' name,
Amen.

Made in the USA
Columbia, SC
05 July 2025

60352738R00029